Baby animals of Asia

Daddy's Stories

I am Yvan the elephant.

I love to spray water with my trunk.

My name is John the orangutan.

I have fun opening coconuts.

I am Jack the red panda.

I jump from branch to branch with great agility.

My name is Gaspard.
I am a snow leopard.

I love playing hide-and-seek in the snow.

I am Ross the rhinoceros.

I enjoy rolling in the mud.

I am Igor the gaur.

I love bathing in rivers.

**My name is Rodger.
I'm a Bengal tiger.**

I need to rest before joining my dad on the hunt.

I am Hope,
the Tibetan antelope.

I love wandering through high-altitude plains.

My name is Vladimir.
I am a Malayan tapir.

My passion is searching for roots in the ground.

My name is Oda the panda.

I spend my days eating bamboo.

I am Merlin the pangolin.

In the afternoon, I love chasing ants.

My name is Oliver.
I am a tarsier.

I spend my time playing in the trees.

Printed in Great Britain
by Amazon